Leave a Breadcrumb…

…Make a Difference

Volume  3

Breadcrumbs from Leviticus

Frances Copeland Lucas

Breadcrumbs from Leviticus
Copyright ©2014 Frances Copeland Lucas
All rights reserved.

This book or parts thereof may not be reproduced in any form, stored in a retrieval system, or transmitted in any form by any means without prior written permission of the authors, except as provided by United States of America copyright law.

Cover Image Credit: http://www.123rf.com/profile_enjoylife25
Cover Design: Elizabeth E. Little, Hyliaan.deviantart.com
Author Website: www.leaveabreadcrumb.com

Little Roni Publishers, LLC
Byhalia, MS

ISBN-13: 978-0692236888
ISBN-10: 0692236880
Also available in eBook publication

BISAC: Religion / Devotional

PRINTED IN THE UNITED STATES OF AMERICA

About Breadcrumbs

Breadcrumbs are small cards to leave behind to help make a difference in your life and the lives of others.

You can get the cards to leave behind everywhere you go for someone else to pick up and read. Each card has a Bible verse or a quote with action steps to take in the areas of Spirituality, Health, Relationships, Career, Finances, and Self-Improvement.

To obtain your free set of Breadcrumbs (the cards), go to www.leaveabreadcrumb.com and sign up for a free set plus two other sets to leave behind. You may also register for the daily devotional email.

This book is dedicated to

the Lord our God who gives us His law, gives us His rules and regulations, gives us His commandments to live by and knows we should obey because He loves us. When we learn His ways, follow and obey Him, we should never have to worry about anything again.

About This Book

While creating Breadcrumbs (the cards), Breadcrumbs devotionals (by email) surfaced which brought about this book.

This book is the second of many books in the series to help readers understand more about the Bible and apply God's word to their lives. This book can be used to make a difference.

How to Use This Book

This book was intended for you to begin or continue a habit of reading God's word, meditating, taking action and noting accomplishments. When we intentionally spend time with God, we will become closer to Him.

Follow these steps to get the most out of this book. Before beginning each day, first pray asking God to show you what He wants you to know from His word. Then…

1. Read the scripture out of your Bible.
2. Read the message from Breadcrumbs.
3. Go over actions steps and take action.
4. Think about the message throughout the day.
5. Write down what God shows you during the day.
6. Ask Him to give you an opportunity to take what you learn and make a difference.

Breadcrumbs from Leviticus

1

HOLD ON TO NOTHING

Read Leviticus 1:1-2

God asked the people to sacrifice what they owned. We must be willing to give to God what we own. It is actually His anyway. God wants us to give Him back what He has given to us as a sacrifice or offering to acknowledge that He alone is holy. We give to God and others because that is what God asks us to do and we should be obedient to Him. We need to be sure we are willing to give God what we own and not hold it higher than we hold Him in our hearts. When we give what we have to God, He will use it to benefit us and others.

ACTION STEPS:

1. List some things you may be holding on to.
2. Ask God to help you learn to let go.
3. Write down some ways you can give what you have to Him.
4. Be ready to give to Him when He asks you to.

MY NOTES

2

OUR BEST

Read Leviticus 1:3-17

God wants our best. He doesn't want second hand things from us. He requires we give Him our best because He is perfect and can only accept our best. When we try our hardest and give everything we have that is good, God accepts it and uses it to bless us and others. When we give half-heartedly and without really trying, God does not accept it and we find ourselves making mistakes. Give your best to God. Allow Him to work through you to be a blessing to you and others.

ACTION STEPS:

1. Write down when you have given your very best.
2. List your skills and your belongings.
3. Ask God to show you how to use them for Him.
4. Trust in Him and take action giving Him your best today.

MY NOTES

3

WE CAN'T PRETEND

Read Leviticus 2:1-7

An offering of grain was presented to thank God for what He has provided to them. God wanted the best of the flour and oil. He knows if we try to give him anything but our best so there is no reason to pretend. We should give our best to God in all we do. When we try to give God our leftovers or short change Him, we won't make a positive difference for Him or others.

ACTION STEPS:

1. Write down what you may be doing that is not your best.
2. List areas where you are simply going through the motions.
3. Ask God to how you can better serve Him.
4. Ask God what you can do to make a positive difference.

MY NOTES

4

BECOME MORE DEVOTED

Read Leviticus 2:8-10

The offering of grain was for the Lord but also for the priests. God took care of them for their faith and loyalty to Him. When we devote our time and all we have to God, He will take care of us. We need not worry about what we have or don't have because when we give God the glory for all we do have, He will take care of all that we need. We need to become more devoted to God with what we do have rather than worry about what we don't have.

ACTION STEPS:

1. Write down some things you believe you need.
2. List what things you are giving to God.
3. Ask God to help you be more devoted to Him with all you have.
4. Look for opportunities to give what you do have to God.

MY NOTES

5

OMITTING THE BAD

Read Leviticus 2:11-12

Omitting yeast was to keep it from going bad. When we add certain ingredients to food, we have to be careful about how long they will last before going bad. In our lives, we have to be sure what we do and who we associate with are not influencing us to do wrong. If we add bad habits and associate with bad people, it won't be long before we begin to do bad things. Sometimes, little by little we could let things slide and before we know it, we are doing things we know are wrong.

ACTION STEPS:

1. Write out some things you do that are wrong in God's eyes.
2. List some things you should eliminate from your life.
3. Go to God daily trusting Him to keep you strong.
4. Thank Him for helping you omit bad things from your life.

MY NOTES

6

ADD SALT

Read Leviticus 2:13

Salt was added as a reminder of God's covenant. It was to show that God was in their lives just as He is in ours. God wants to be part of everything we do and we need to present Him with all of our situations, good or bad. He is there for us to praise in the struggles and in the celebrations. We need to remember to add God to all areas of our lives so He can bring out what needs to be revealed so we can make a difference. God wants us to glorify Him in all we do.

ACTION STEPS:

1. Write down an area of your life where you are struggling.
2. List how you have added God to this part of your life.
3. What actions are you taking that God is not a part of?
4. Ask God to help you with this and to know what He wants you to do.

MY NOTES

7

MAKE A BLESSING

Read Leviticus 2:14-16

As they prepared their harvest, they took the first portion and made it ready for an offering and that pleased God. When we are doing anything from cooking to making plans for our weekend, we need to give it to God. He will take that first portion of our time, money, talents and make a blessing from them. Anyone of any age, culture or poverty level can give God the first and best of what they have. We need to examine what we do and be sure we are allowing God to make a blessing.

ACTION STEPS:

1. Write down what you things you do all day.
2. List the things you do that you specifically give to God.
3. Ask God to help you remember to give Him the first of all you do.
4. Trust in God to make a blessing with what you give Him.

MY NOTES

8

FIND PEACE

Read Leviticus 3:1

People had to present an offering to God to find peace. This sacrifice was a gesture to God showing they were grateful to Him and wanted a relationship with Him. We can now find peace in Jesus as our Lord and Savior. We can pray to God without giving anything we have. However, if we do give to Him, we can find a greater peace because we are doing His will as a gesture to Him. We are showing we are grateful to Him and want a relationship with Him.

ACTION STEPS:

1. Write down what you are doing to give to God and others.
2. List three things can you do or give as a gesture of gratitude.
3. Look for opportunities to give today to someone in need.
4. Give some time to God today and ask Him to help you find peace.

MY NOTES

9

GIVE WITH YOUR HEART

Read Leviticus 3:1, 6, 12

The sacrifice of peace could be from their herd, flock or a goat. It didn't matter what they chose to give. The act of giving is what mattered. Giving a part of us or giving something we have is what matters. God blesses us with many things and when we give to others from what we are blessed with, we do find the ultimate peace that God can give to us. It doesn't matter what we give if we give sincerely with our hearts.

ACTION STEPS:

1. Write down how and when you give.
2. List some of the reasons you give.
3. Ask God to show you what to give and when.
4. Be sure when you give you are giving with your heart.

MY NOTES

10

ONE THING TO GIVE

Read Leviticus 3:5, 11, 16

The people were asked to give their offerings. The priests sprinkled the blood and burnt the offerings. The priests helped the people to give their offerings to God. Sometimes when we give we need help from others. We may just have one thing to give but someone else may have the talents to use that one thing to be a blessing to someone else. We aren't required to know everything or be able to do everything. We are just asked to give what we have and let God work with it as He wishes.

ACTION STEPS:

1. Forget about the things you don't have and don't know.
2. Write down what you do have to give and what you know.
3. List some ways to get others involved in your giving.
4. Ask God to help you find others who you can team up with to help someone.

MY NOTES

11

BE WILLING TO FORGIVE

Read Leviticus 4

Sometimes we sin without realizing it but sometimes it is intentional. God allows us to come to Him and ask for forgiveness. It is when we realize that we have sinned and come to Him that we grow. He is a just and forgiving God and His mercy shows because He is willing to forgive. We must be willing to forgive others for their sins as well because God made us in His image and if He can forgive, we can too.

ACTION STEPS:

1. Make a list of those you need to forgive.
2. Write down the situation and why are you are upset.
3. Ask God to help you to forgive.
4. Show the love God wants you to show to them through forgiveness.

MY NOTES

12

RELEASE THE GUILT

Read Leviticus 5

When we sin, we should acknowledge that sin before God asking Him to forgive us. Guilt comes from sin and our guilt can keep us from doing what we need to do for God. We can release that guilt when we allow God to forgive us. He forgets our sins and wipes our slate clean so we don't have to feel guilty. However, if we hold on to that sin our guilt becomes unbearable. We need to let go of our sins and ask for forgiveness so we can do the things God wants us to do.

ACTION STEPS:

1. Write down some sins you may be holding on to.
2. List the things do you feel most guilty about.
3. Ask God to forgive you for your sins.
4. Ask Him to help you release the guilt so you can better do His will.

MY NOTES

13

NOTHING ORDINARY

Read Leviticus 6

God gave the people further instructions about offerings. If they just did what they had to do to get by, it would not be acceptable to God. We have to be sure what we are doing is not just to get by. We tithe just what we are asked to. We help just when we are asked to. We read the Bible because we are supposed to. We have to be sure we are doing these things for the right reasons. We have to be willing to do more than what is asked of us and wait for further instructions from God. He will give us give more to do and wants us to be more than we think we can. There is nothing ordinary about God so what He wants us to do is not going to be ordinary either.

ACTION STEPS:

1. Write down some things you have been doing in your life.
2. Mark off which things are expected of you.
3. Ask God to help you do more.
4. Remember He is not ordinary and His requests may not be either.

MY NOTES

14

WHEN WE ARE CLEAN

Read Leviticus 7:1-10

The guilt offering was the most holy. When we are guilty of something and we go to God for forgiveness, we are cleansed of our sin. When we are clean, we are able to be closer to God. When we are closer to God, we can better understand His word, serve Him more and help others. That is why it is important to remove the wood out of our own eye before we try to help someone else as the scriptures say in Matthew 7:5.

ACTION STEPS:

1. List some things you feel guilty about.
2. Write down why they are hindering you from God.
3. Ask God to forgive you for dwelling on these things.
4. Thank Him for cleansing you and work to move closer to Him.

MY NOTES

15

PEACE THROUGH OFFERINGS

Read Leviticus 7:11-21

There were three types of peace offerings. There were offerings of thanksgiving, offerings to fulfill a vow and freewill offerings. We can find peace when we offer thanksgiving to God. We can find peace when we know we are doing God's will. We can find peace when we just sit and meditate on His word. However, the Bible says these offerings were temporary. That is why we should continually look for peace and not make one gesture of offering every once in a while. God's peace is everlasting and we need His peace every day of our lives.

ACTION STEPS:

1. List some offerings you have given in the past to God.
2. Write down what other types of offerings can you give.
3. Ask God to show you how to continuously give.
4. Allow God to work in you to have peace through offerings.

MY NOTES

16

JUST BECAUSE

Read Leviticus 7:22-27

God gave them exact instructions about what not to eat. We see later in the Bible He doesn't forget what He commanded them to do. People were put to death many years later for not obeying what their ancestors were instructed to do. Although times have changed, God's law has not. We should be sure we are not trying to bend God's law to conform to the world just because there are so many people doing things out of God's will. We can set the example and be reminders to others what God's law is and has always been.

ACTION STEPS:

1. List some things others do out of God's will.
2. Ask God to help you know what is right and wrong in His eyes.
3. Write down some ways you can set the example to do right.
4. Look for opportunities to share God's way with others.

MY NOTES

17

LOOKING FOR PEACE

Read Leviticus 7:28-30

The people were asked to present the peace offering to the Lord themselves. God cannot give us peace unless we go to Him directly. We can't get it from other means. Real peace comes from God directly to us through His word, through our communication to and from Him and by knowing Jesus as our personal Savior. Looking for peace by any other means is pointless.

ACTION STEPS:

1. Write out the areas you need peace in your life.
2. Ask God to help you find peace through Him.
3. Read His word and pray directly for His peace.
4. Go to Him daily; build a relationship to know Him and to know His peace.

MY NOTES

18

OUR FAITHFUL LEADERS

Read Leviticus 7:31-36

A share of the offering was to be for the priest. The priests were committed to God and God took care of them in His way. We need to hold high our leaders in faith and give to them as if we are giving to God. They are committed in a way we may never know. When we give to them, we give to God. When we give to God, He ensures they are taken care of so they can continue on doing His will without the worries of meeting their daily needs themselves.

ACTION STEPS:

1. List some women and men of God who you know.
2. Ask God to show you how you can give to them and help them.
3. Tell them you appreciate them and their dedication to God.
4. Look for opportunities to help them carry out God's plan for them.

MY NOTES

19

MORE TO GIVE

Read Leviticus 7:37-38

The people gave an offering as a way for them to remember what they had done and what they wanted to do. It was an action of faith on their part and a request to God to bless them. They had to take action to make these offerings to God. We have to take action if we want blessings from God, too. We can't just expect to be blessed when we are doing nothing for Him or for others. God wants us to present offerings to Him out of obedience, honor and respect for who He is. We can do this by giving to Him our time, talents and treasures and by helping others while giving God the glory for what He has given to us. He will bless us with more and then we will have more to give.

ACTION STEPS:

1. Think of some ways you can give to God and others.
2. Write down some things you can do today.
3. Ask God to show you opportunities to give and take action.
4. Do something every day and look for God's blessings to share with others.

MY NOTES

20

BE CLEANSED

Read Leviticus 8:34

Aaron and his sons had to be cleansed and made holy before they could help other people. We can't help others if we aren't doing the right things. We need to be sure we are cleansed and renewed daily by God so we can help others and be a blessing as God wants us to be. He can't work through an unclean heart.

ACTION STEPS:

1. Write down what part of your life needs to be cleansed.
2. Ask God to forgive you and make you right with Him.
3. Go to God daily to be renewed and cleansed.
4. Ask God to work through you so you can help others.

MY NOTES

21

TITLES ARE NOT ENOUGH

Read Leviticus 8:35-36

They were set apart from the other men by the rituals so they would be holy and cleansed spiritually. Their title alone was not enough for them to be cleansed. If we have a certain title in the church or at work that doesn't mean that we are automatically able to do the job. We have to go through procedures and learn things that will help us to do the job better. Titles alone don't make us who we are. It's what's inside us that God wants to use so we can help others.

ACTION STEPS:

1. List your titles and roles in life.
2. Think about your values and what you actually do.
3. Ask God to help you examine if you are doing all you can.
4. Look for ways to improve and remember titles aren't everything.

MY NOTES

22

WHEN AND THEN

Read Leviticus 9:1-7

When you do this then you will be blessed. Moses told Aaron when you do these things, then your people will be blessed and you will see the Lord. We have to take the action God is asking us to do, then we will see His blessings move through us. When we read the Bible more, then we greater understand God's plan for us. When we help a neighbor, then God blesses us and them. When we take initiative, then we are given more. When we give to others, then we are given back tenfold. What is your when?

ACTION STEPS:

1. List some things God has been calling you to do.
2. Write down what things are holding you back.
3. Ask God to help you move forward and do His will.
4. When God shows you how to take the first step, take it.

MY NOTES

23

WITHOUT ACTION

Read Leviticus 9:8-20

Without the action, the blessing may not come. If the blessings do not come, others may not be blessed either. Aaron and his sons had to take action in faith for their people to see the miracle God planned for them. If they decided not do it, the people would not have seen the fire consume the burnt offering and the fat. If the people would not have seen it, they would not have received the joy and been able to worship God in His presence.

ACTION STEPS:

1. Write down what actions you have been putting off for God.
2. Think about who has missed out because of this.
3. Ask God to help you take the action He wants you to take.
4. Look for ways to get started today to do what God calls you to do.

MY NOTES

24

GET READY FOR THE LORD

Read Leviticus 9:21-24

Moses told Aaron what to do to prepare for the Lord. We have to get ready if we want to worship Him as well. We will get much more out of our worship if we prepare ourselves ahead of time. We can do this by prayer. We can do this by realizing how great God is in the scope of all the universe. We can do this by a favorite scripture or in song. We need to prepare and be ready.

ACTION STEPS:

1. Decide if you are really ready for the Lord today.
2. Write out how your mindset is right now.
3. Are you worried or anxious about anything?
4. Ask God to allow the Holy Spirit to show you how to prepare for worship.

MY NOTES

25

CAREFUL AND OBEDIENT

Read Leviticus 10:1-3

Carelessness or disobedience is not tolerated by God. When He gives us something to do, we should be careful and obedient. We must do what God asks us to do and not alter His direction. Sometimes when we rush to get things done trying to be obedient to God, we miss something very important. Take time, the first time, to do what God asks you to do. Don't rush through His word or through a prayer. He wants us to be careful and obedient.

ACTION STEPS:

1. Write down the last time you talked with God.
2. Were you rushing or did you take your time?
3. What things have you rushed through lately for God?
4. Ask God to help you slow down and be careful while you do His work.

MY NOTES

26

HOLD IT!

Read Leviticus 10:4-7

Aaron's others sons were told not to outwardly mourn for their brothers or the people would suffer. Leaders sometimes have to hold their emotions in as an example to those who follow them. They have to be neutral on some issues so not to sway people in one direction or another. Supporting what God wants us to do requires we sometimes hold in our emotions around others. It is not always easy, but it is a requirement so we can be a godly example to others.

ACTION STEPS:

1. Write about a time you let your emotions out.
2. What was the situation and the outcome?
3. Could you have handled it differently and produced different results?
4. Ask God to help you control your emotions and be a better example to others.

MY NOTES

27

CHOOSE NOT TO DRINK

Read Leviticus 10:8-11

Alcohol does alter things. Outwardly it shows that people are in need of the things of the world rather than being dependent on God to relax and enjoy life. Inwardly it messes up our bodies if we abuse it. Also, it blurs our thinking and slurs our words. We must be careful of what example we are showing to others when we choose to drink alcohol. We also should be careful of what we put in our bodies.

ACTION STEPS:

1. List some people you know someone who enjoys drinking alcohol.
2. Write down how alcohol has or has not impacted your life.
3. Allow God to help you be an example to others in this area.
4. Ask God to show you how to help others choose not to drink.

MY NOTES

28

WE DON'T ALWAYS KNOW

Read Leviticus 10:12-20

Moses, at first, didn't understand why the brothers would not eat the sin offering until Aaron explained the situation. We don't always understand why things happen because we don't know the whole story. Sometimes we may never know. That is why we should have an open mind and not try to determine if what someone did was right or wrong in our eyes and let God be the judge of it.

ACTION STEPS:

1. Write about a time where you didn't know the whole situation.
2. Write down if you asked questions or just got upset and over-reacted.
3. Were you able to let things go and let God be the Judge?
4. Ask God to help you know when to ask and know when to let things go.

MY NOTES

29

STAY AWAY

Read Leviticus 11

The people were to stay away from things that were unclean. God wants us to stay away from things that will make us unclean as well. When we go to places where it is easy to be tempted and hang around people who do things against God's will, it may be hard to resist to do the right things. Staying away, on purpose, from things of the world that are against God is the best way to do the right thing. However, that doesn't mean that we shouldn't witness to those who are not in the will of God. It does mean we don't need to do what they do and live as they live.

ACTION STEPS:

1. List some places you have to go where you could possibly be tempted.
2. Ask God to help you resist temptation when you are there.
3. Write down ways to be a better witness to others in those places.
4. Ask God for strength when you are in those places so you can do His will.

MY NOTES

30

DON'T MOVE AWAY

Read Leviticus 11

If the people did things to remain unclean, they would not be ready to worship God at any time. When we do things we shouldn't, we may move away from God for short periods in our life and not worship Him as we should. Sometimes we move away for years because we are ashamed at first but then it becomes habit to be out of the will of God. We must be ready to worship God at all times. That is why we need to stay away from the things of the world that are not pleasing to Him.

ACTION STEPS:

1. Write about some things you are doing that are not God's will.
2. Write down when and why you did them.
3. Have you moved away from God because of these things?
4. Ask God to bring you closer to Him and help you get back into His will.

MY NOTES

31

WHAT IS WRONG?

Read Leviticus 12:1-7

Something as wonderful as childbirth left the women unclean before God. They were unprepared to go with an offering until their bodies were completely clean. Our God is so holy He requires every part of us be clean no matter what the circumstances were which made us unclean. There may be something in our lives right now we think is okay but may be unclean to God. Ask God to reveal to you any part of your life that may not be as He wants it to be.

ACTION STEPS:

1. Write down things around you and see what things may not be pleasing to God.
2. List some thoughts and words you say that may not be right with God.
3. Ask God to reveal to you anything in your life you need to get rid of.
4. Ask God to show you how to remove what is bad from your life today.

MY NOTES

32

REPLACE WORLDLY WITH HIS WORD

Read Leviticus 12:8

Worship should be done when we can set aside all the things of the world and are able to completely focus on God and His godliness. If we have something distracting us it will be harder to focus on Him. Unclean doesn't always mean sin or dirt. Unclean could mean things of the world. If the things of the world are on our minds when we go to worship, how can we truly talk and listen to God? We must remove those things and come to Him with an open heart and mind.

ACTION STEPS:

1. List some things that have been on your mind.
2. Write down how it is keeping you from worship.
3. Go to God and ask Him to help you set the world aside.
4. Ask God to replace your worldly thoughts with His word and worship Him.

MY NOTES

33

PUTTING OUR SINS BEHIND US

Read Leviticus 13

Since Jesus had not yet been born, cleanliness on the outside was important in those days. But now we can ask for forgiveness from God and know Jesus cleansed us from our sins through His death on the cross. Is there something in our lives that needs cleansed? We can't really do any good for God or anyone else, even ourselves, if we go around unclean in God's eyes. It's time we put our sins behind us so we can do good for God.

ACTION STEPS:

1. List some things you have done that are wrong.
2. Write down what you need to remove in your life that is sin.
3. Ask God to forgive you and allow you to be cleansed.
4. Seek out ways to do good for God, others and yourself and put your sins behind you.

MY NOTES

34

BE WELL

Read Leviticus 14:1-32

God wants us to stay healthy. Sometimes we have sickness and disease and we are not sure of the cause. We just have to do what is right to get better and trust in God to handle the rest. However, some of us do things that cause us to be unhealthy with bad habits that hurt our bodies and minds. We need to be mindful of what we are doing to our bodies and what we are putting into our bodies so we are sure to treat our bodies as God wants us to. We need to be sure we are doing all we can to take care of our bodies so we can do our work for God.

ACTION STEPS:

1. Write down how your health has been over the years.
2. List some things you have done to keep good health.
3. Are there any things you need to stop doing?
4. Ask God to help you take better care of yourself starting today.

MY NOTES

35

BETTER PREPARE

Read Leviticus 14:33-57

Just as our bodies need to be clean because Jesus lives inside of them, our homes need to be clean as well. Before God even gave the homes to the people, He instructed them what to do if they were unclean. God sees the things ahead of us and wants us to know how to handle them. We can prepare for what is ahead through prayer and reading His word. What is God telling you to do to better prepare your body and home for Him?

ACTION STEPS:

1. Write down what you see around your home.
2. List the things you do regularly and what you put in your body.
3. Ask God to reveal to you what to get rid of and hang on to.
4. Do what God wants and use your home and body for His purpose.

MY NOTES

36

STAY HEALTHY

Read Leviticus 15

The instructions about bodily discharges were to protect the people. God looks out for us and wants us to be careful about passing on diseases to each other. He gives us instructions on how to care for each other. We must be sure we keep from passing germs to others and recognize when we are not feeling well, we may be contagious. Being aware of how we are feeling does have an impact on others and we are here to be our brother's keeper. We should take care of ourselves and be sure we take care of others as well.

ACTION STEPS:

1. Write down some things about your own personal health.
2. List those who you know with health problems.
3. Ask God to help you to take care of your body.
4. Ask God to help you be an example for others to stay healthy.

MY NOTES

37

DAILY RENEW YOURSELF

Read Leviticus 16

Aaron was responsible for taking the steps of purification for him, his family and the people of Israel. This was a huge responsibility. We are only responsible for ourselves and that is a great task by itself. To stay pure, there is a constant renewal of prayer and repentance of sin. We die daily as Paul says so we have to renew ourselves daily with God. Find your time of purification to daily renew yourself so you can be a role model to others giving God all the glory.

ACTION STEPS:

1. Write down the last time you renewed with repentance and prayer.
2. List some things you need to go to God about where you have sinned.
3. Confess your sins and ask God to forgive you.
4. Thank God for His goodness and remember throughout the day you have been renewed.

MY NOTES

38

COMPLETE DEPENDENCE

Read Leviticus 17

The Lord gave specific rules about where to sacrifice the animals and what to do with the blood. The people who obeyed showed their faithfulness to him. God said He would turn against anyone who drank the blood in any form. These rules were made for the people to show their faith and help them to have complete dependence on God. When we try to do things our own way and not God's way we move away from Him and His glory. We become dependent on other things and not Him. We can only be close to God when we are doing what He tells us to do.

ACTION STEPS:

1. List some things you have done lately.
2. Write down if these things were what God wanted or what you wanted.
3. Do you depend on yourself, on others or on God?
4. Ask God to help you be completely dependent on Him and to help you follow His will.

MY NOTES

39

NOT AS POPULAR

Read Leviticus 18:1-23

We are not to succumb to practices of others in any part of the world that are not in line with what God wants us to do. God's will is not always the most popular thing to do. However, we must remain strong knowing that He alone is God and will be with us in anything we do if we are doing His will. When we step away from Him to hang with the crowd, we are setting ourselves up for trouble. We must follow His ways in order to do what He has planned for us even when it is not so popular with the world to do so.

ACTION STEPS:

1. Think and pray about what God wants you to do.
2. Write down what are you doing now in line with His will.
3. List some things should you stop doing.
4. Ask God to help you to take a stand today to do His will and not what others want you to do.

MY NOTES

40

CONTROL THE URGES

Read Leviticus 18:24-30

People get urges to do things sometimes because they are in the wrong place doing the wrong thing. Sexual sin comes from the devil who puts those desires in humans to try something different or to lust after someone they are not married to. We have to decide before we are put in any situation that we are not going to sin against God with our bodies. It is best to stay away from those situations all together; however, if we have the mindset not to do those things ahead of time and ask God for strength, He will guide us through those temptations.

ACTION STEPS:

1. Write down an urge you have had or are having.
2. Write about the situation and why it happened.
3. Ask God to forgive you for your actions and thoughts.
4. Ask God to help you to have the mindset that will help you control these urges in the future.

MY NOTES

41

NO GRAY AREA

Read Leviticus 19:1-36

God reminds us that He is holy. He reminds us about His laws. We see His laws repeated throughout the Bible and how great He is. These constant reminders are not for Him but for us to know that His law doesn't change no matter what others say. We shouldn't look for excuses on how these laws don't really apply to us or how we can bend them because the world has changed. God's laws still apply to us and there is no gray area. We either obey them or we don't.

ACTION STEPS:

1. Read over these laws God has given us.
2. Write down ways you can be more obedient to God.
3. Ask God to help you to be more obedient.
4. As you go through the day, remember God's laws.

MY NOTES

42

WE NEED GOD

Read Leviticus 19:37

The last verse in the chapter says we must obey all of his laws and put them into practice. This doesn't mean to tell others what they should or shouldn't do. This means we need to obey and not just talk being obedient and how others should do the same. We need to examine our lives and our actions to be sure we measure up to who God wants us to be. If we are not doing these things, we need to go to Him to help us because we can't do good on our own. We need God.

ACTION STEPS:

1. Write down God's laws and think about how they apply to you.
2. List your actions in these areas and write about what you need to change.
3. Ask God to help you to live as He wants you to.
4. Allow God to work through you and help you when you are tempted to do wrong.

MY NOTES

43

BEYOND OUR IMAGINATION

Read Leviticus 20

God tells us we should not put our trust and hope in other people. When we try to find happiness or seek fulfillment through another person, we will not truly be happy. God is all we need for happiness and fulfillment. When we seek Him and obey His laws, we will see the things of the world are only temporary. We will see all people are human and make mistakes so we can't rely on them like we can depend on God. His laws are to help us serve Him better and our obedience to Him will give us opportunities beyond our imagination.

ACTION STEPS:

1. Write down the names of those who have let you down.
2. List some things they did you felt were wrong.
3. Know that God will never disappoint you and ask Him how you can serve Him.
4. Look for ways to serve God and expect great things from Him.

MY NOTES

44

REMOVE THE SIN

Read Leviticus 21:1-21

God said those who were imperfect should not approach Him. He wasn't saying that He didn't love them. Because He is so holy, only people without imperfections on their skin could be near Him and only certain animals could be sacrificed. Our God is holy and needs to be respected as such. If we are unclean, we must remove the sin by asking His forgiveness before we can have the right relationship with Him.

ACTION STEPS:

1. Are you trying to talk to God but feel He isn't listening?
2. Write down something in your life that could be sin.
3. Ask God to forgive you for this sin and help you to move on.
4. Go to God and ask Him to help you strengthen your relationship with Him.

MY NOTES

45

TALENTS AND GIFTS

Read Leviticus 21:22-24

Although some were not able to approach God, they still had other responsibilities and were able to worship Him by using their talents and gifts He gave them in different ways. We all can't be priests or preachers. It takes people from all walks of life to make this world go around. We must not focus on what we don't have but instead focus on what God has blessed us with and use that for His glory!

ACTION STEPS:

1. Write down how much time you spend dwelling on what you don't have.
2. Make a list of all the talents and gifts you do have.
3. Ask God to help you focus on what you have rather than what you don't.
4. Look for ways to use your talents and gifts as God wants you to.

MY NOTES

46

DECIDE TO BE CLEAN

Read Leviticus 22:1-30

Was it really that different back then than it is now? The rituals have changed but our God has not. He is still holy and wants our best in all we do. When we are around uncleanliness it makes us unclean but we have the blood of Jesus to wash away our sins and make us clean again. We must remember God can't be around unclean things but through our choices we can be clean by giving our best to Him. Then we can be with Him daily so He can take care of us and use us to do His will for us.

ACTION STEPS:

1. Write down the things you do which may not be pleasing to God.
2. Ask Him to help you identify and remove those things from your life.
3. Go to God for forgiveness and allow Him to change your ways.
4. Look for new things to replace your old ways so you can be clean and obey God.

MY NOTES

47

GOD DOES THE HARD PART

Read Leviticus 22:31-33

We are ordinary. God is not. He is faithful. Sometimes we are not. He gave us His son so we may be closer to Him. As He rescued the Israelites from Egypt, He has rescued us from hell. We are asked to obey Him and be faithful. He does the hard part because He is good at it. We have to just do what we are told. That isn't always easy but nothing is really easy at first; however, we have God to guide us and when we have faith and obey, He will give us what we need to make it easier to do His will.

ACTION STEPS:

1. Write down what God is asking you to do.
2. List anything that has kept you from doing it.
3. Ask God to help you know the next step to take.
4. Obey Him and step out in faith today to do His will.

MY NOTES

48

HOLD ON AND REMEMBER

Read Leviticus 23:1-4

It is so easy to take forget the true reason for the Sabbath and other holidays where we should really stop and remember why we celebrate them. The Sabbath is to rest from work and remember God. The other holidays are for celebration and remembrance. Let's not forget the past that God wants us so desperately to hold on to and remember. There is a reason we have these days of rest and celebration. Don't take them lightly.

ACTION STEPS:

1. Write about the reasons you celebrate holidays.
2. List what things do you normally do during the holidays.
3. Ask God to help you make Him a part of your celebration.
4. Remember to keep the Sabbath holy and God in all of your holidays.

MY NOTES

49

GOD CONTINUES

Read Leviticus 23:5-44

Their special days were designed to help them remember what God had done for them and continued to do. Their deliverance, their food, their blessings, their harvest, their fellowship and God's continued guidance came from God. We don't need a holiday to thank God for these things daily. We should remember how great He is in everything we do. We need to give Him the glory for the great things He has done, long ago, and what He continues to do in our lives. He never stops. He never changes. He just continues to be great.

ACTION STEPS:

1. Write down the last time you really thought about how great God is.
2. Read over the scripture and know God is in your life in all these areas as well.
3. Ask God to help you remember His greatness throughout the day and week.
4. List ways to acknowledge Him and tell others about how He continues to be great in your life.

MY NOTES

50

DO WHAT IS RIGHT

Read Leviticus 24:10-21

God doesn't take His laws lightly and neither should we. We need to be careful about what we say and what we do. Just because someone else does something or we see people do things on television doesn't mean God has changed his mind. We are to be as He has commanded us to be. We are to honor and respect Him and love others. We can't be who He wants us to be without Him. We can be with Him if we don't obey. We can show Him we are ready to follow Him by obeying His word and using His strength to do what is right.

ACTION STEPS:

1. List the laws you know that are God's laws.
2. What laws do you take lightly?
3. What laws has the world stopped obeying?
4. Ask God to give you His strength to obey and do what is right.

MY NOTES

51

PREPARE AND BE FAITHFUL

Read Leviticus 25:1-22

God was giving Moses plans for the future. He told him what to tell the people to do over the next 50 years to prepare for a celebration. That is a long time to prepare and be faithful for something wonderful to happen. However, that is what we are to do on earth. We are to ask God for His plans for us and be faithful until our time of celebration with Him when we get to heaven. What is God asking you to do to prepare and be faithful in for the future?

ACTION STEPS:

1. Write down the plans you have for life.
2. List some things you know God is calling you to do.
3. Ask God to guide you to do what He wants and not what you want.
4. Prepare to do what God wants and be faithful to Him.

MY NOTES

52

IT'S NOT OURS

Read Leviticus 25:23-34

Although there were rules about buying and selling property, God wanted the people to know all the land belonged to Him. We should remember nothing on this earth is ours and we need to take care of it and be willing to share what we use with others. God is the owner of all things on earth and in heaven. What we have belongs to Him and we need to thank Him for what He provides to us.

ACTION STEPS:

1. Write down what you believe is yours.
2. Remember it is not yours at all but belongs to God.
3. Ask God how you can use what you have to help others.
4. List ways to help others with what God has blessed you with.

MY NOTES

53

HELPING OTHERS

Read Leviticus 25:35-55

Taking care of others was important back in those days just as it is now. There are many people struggling who need our help. When we choose to focus only on us and just our immediate area then we are not doing what God asks us to do. We need to reach out to help the poor and those who can't help themselves or do anything for us in return.

ACTION STEPS:

1. Write down where you spend most of your time.
2. Is it more on what you want for yourself or to help others?
3. Ask God to show you what you can do more of for others.
4. Look for opportunities to help others in everything you do.

MY NOTES

54

OBEDIENCE OR DISOBEDIENCE

Read Leviticus 26:1-22

Freedom or captivity, peace or disaster, Joy or unhappiness? The Israelites had these choices just as we do. We can choose to be obedient doing what God has called us to do or we can choose to do things our own way and live with the consequences. God gives us the outcome of our choices between obedience and disobedience. It's our decision.

ACTION STEPS:

1. Write down where you are being obedient to God.
2. List the things you do which are disobedient.
3. Ask God what changes you need to make to obey God.
4. Look for ways to do His will rather than your own today.

MY NOTES

55

DO WHAT IS RIGHT

Read Leviticus 26:23-39

When we have the opportunity to do what is right, why would we want to do what is wrong? We have choices. Doing what is right brings so many good things to others and to us. When we do things wrong, we live in sin, hurt others and disobey God. It feels so good to do the right thing. Why would anyone want to do anything else?

ACTION STEPS:

1. Write out your actions yesterday.
2. List which of them would please God.
3. Ask Him to help you do what pleases Him today.
4. Pray throughout the day as a reminder to do what is right.

MY NOTES

56

RETURN TO HIM

Read Leviticus 26:40-46

God tells us He will not totally reject us. He is waiting for us to call on Him when we do mess up after trying to do things our own way. That doesn't mean we have His permission to go and do things on our own. It means He is a loving, just and forgiving god. He knows we are human and will sometimes take the wrong turn. And He wants us to know He is waiting for us to return to Him.

ACTION STEPS:

1. List your recent mistakes or when you took a wrong turn.
2. Write about the situation and the result.
3. Did you go to God for help?
4. Return to God today and ask Him to forgive and help you.

MY NOTES

57

SET IT APART AS HOLY

Read Leviticus 27:1-32

All that we have is the Lord's; however, He wants us to give Him back a portion of it. We are to set it apart to Him as holy. When we give our offerings to the Lord, do we do it with good will? Or do we do it just as we pay our bills thinking about what we could do with that money if we kept it? Next time you give, remember you are setting apart a portion of what you have to God as holy. Pray about your giving and what it will be used for.

ACTION STEPS:

1. Write down what you last gave to God.
2. Put the date on it and why you gave.
3. Think about your frame of mind when you gave.
4. Ask God to help you give setting it apart as holy for Him.

MY NOTES

58

OUR FIRST AND OUR BEST

Read Leviticus 27:33-34

Remember our act of giving is in remembrance of Him and in obedience to Him. He doesn't tell us to give if we can. He tells us to give our first and our best to Him. He does not want our last and our worst. Our God is perfect in every way and He uses our gifts whether it is our treasures, talents or time. He won't use them if our attitude isn't right about it and He won't use them if we don't give our best.

ACTION STEPS:

1. Write down what portion you give to God.
2. List anything that is keeping you from giving as you should.
3. Ask God to give you strength to give as He asks you to.
4. Create a new habit of giving your first and your best to God.

MY NOTES

Leave a Breadcrumb...
   ...make a difference!

About the Author

Frances Lucas has lived in Birmingham, Alabama for over 40 years. She is a working mother with three "should be grown" children and has progressively improved her life through mistakes, persistence, and a sense of humor. Her passion in life surfaced after major setbacks in life which proved to her that good things can come from bad experiences.

She believes God's purpose for her life is to share her experiences and help others to learn from their mistakes so they can be who God wants them to be and serve both Him and others.

Her website, www.leaveabreadcrumb.com, is her way of wanting to make a difference along with the creation of her first book - *Breadcrumbs from Genesis*. Frances is a Christian coach who also coaches in career development and personal improvement, facilitates self-improvement classes, and enjoys writing. She has a daily devotional email sent from her Breadcrumbs website.

Contact Frances at frances@leavebreadcrumb.com or visit her site http://www.francescopelandlucas.com/ to sign up for a free daily devotional or her Breadcrumb site to get your free introductory set of Breadcrumbs.

More Non-Fiction from Little Roni Publishers

You CAN Self-Publish and *You CAN Self-Promote*
by Author/Speaker Ellen C. Maze
$10 paperback / $2.99 Kindle
www.amazon.com
www.LittleRoniPublishers.com

Check out other devotionals by Frances Copeland Lucas:

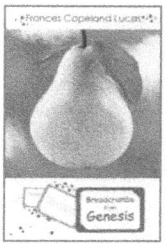

Breadcrumbs from Genesis Begin your journey through the Bible in Genesis, studying God's word one chapter at a time. Each day has a scripture, how it applies to your life and action steps to take. There is a place each day to capture your thoughts and journal about your day.

Breadcrumbs from Exodus Continue your journey through the Bible in Exodus, studying God's word one chapter at a time. Each day has a scripture, how it applies to your life and action steps to take. There is a place each day to capture your thoughts and journal about your day.

30 Days of Making a Difference Start each day with God's word, how it applies to your life. The Bible is filled with stories that teach us how we can live each day. Take 30 days to immerse yourself in God's word and look for ways to make a difference.

Breadcrumbs on Wisdom Wisdom from the Bible is the best wisdom we can obtain. Take the next 31 days to immerse yourself seeking God's wisdom.

www.francescopelandlucas.com

www.ingramcontent.com/pod-product-compliance
Lightning Source LLC
Chambersburg PA
CBHW060807050426
42449CB00008B/1578